Global FastFood Delights

Recipe Collection For International Flavors

mahdi amini

Recipe

World Foods:

1. **North American Classics:**

    - Hamburger

    - Cheeseburger

    - Hot Dog

    - French Fries

    - Buffalo Wings

    - Philly Cheesesteak

    - Poutine (Canada)

2. **South American Flavors:**

    - Empanadas

    - Arepas (Venezuela)

    - Ceviche (Peru)

    - Tamales (Mexico)

3. **European Treats:**

    - Fish and Chips (UK)

    - Croissant Sandwich (France)

    - Gyros (Greece)

    - Italian Gelato

4. **Asian Delights:**

    - Sushi (Japan)

    - Ramen (Japan)

    - Dim Sum (China)

    - Thai Green Curry

    - Biryani (India)

5. **Middle Eastern Eats:**

    - Shawarma

- Falafel
- Hummus

6. **African Specialties:**
   - Bunny Chow (South Africa)
   - Suya (Nigeria)

7. **Australian and Oceania Tastes:**
   - Meat Pie (Australia)
   - Lamingtons (Australia)

8. **Caribbean Cuisine:**
   - Jamaican Jerk Chicken
   - Roti (Trinidad and Tobago)

9. **Miscellaneous Favorites:**
   - Sausage Roll (UK/Australia)
   - Samgyeopsal (Korean BBQ)

Classic Hamburger

Ingredients:

- 1 pound (450g) ground beef (80% lean, 20% fat)
- 4 hamburger buns
- 4 slices of American cheese (optional)
- 1/2 cup lettuce, shredded
- 1/2 cup tomatoes, sliced
- 1/4 cup red onions, thinly sliced
- Pickles (optional)
- Ketchup and mustard
- Salt and black pepper to taste

Instructions:

1. **Prepare the Grill:** Preheat your grill to high heat or heat a grill pan on the stovetop.
2. **Form the Patties:** Divide the ground beef into four equal portions. Gently shape each portion into a patty, about 1 inch thick. Avoid overworking the meat to keep it tender.
3. **Season the Patties:** Sprinkle salt and black pepper on both sides of each patty.
4. **Grill the Patties:** Place the patties on the grill or grill pan. Cook for about 3-4 minutes per side for medium-rare or longer for your preferred level of doneness. If using cheese, add a slice to each patty during the last minute of cooking and cover the grill to melt it.
5. **Toast the Buns:** While the patties are cooking, split the hamburger buns and toast them lightly on the grill until they become slightly crispy.
6. **Assemble the Burgers:** Place a lettuce leaf on the bottom half of each bun, followed by a tomato slice, red onion slices, and pickles if desired. Place the cooked patty with or without melted cheese on top.
7. **Add Condiments:** Squeeze ketchup and mustard on the patty or customize with your preferred condiments.
8. **Complete the Burger:** Top with the other half of the bun. You can use a toothpick to hold it all together if needed.
9. **Serve:** Serve the hamburgers with a side of french fries or onion rings.

Enjoy your homemade classic hamburgers! Feel free to adjust the toppings and condiments to your taste.

Cheeseburger

Ingredients:

For the Burger Patties:

- 1 pound (450g) ground beef (80% lean, 20% fat)
- Salt and black pepper to taste

For the Cheeseburgers:

- 4 hamburger buns
- 4 slices of American cheese (or your preferred cheese)
- 1/2 cup lettuce, shredded
- 1/2 cup tomatoes, sliced
- 1/4 cup red onions, thinly sliced
- Pickles (optional)
- Ketchup and mustard (or your preferred condiments)

Instructions:

1. **Prepare the Grill or Pan:** Preheat your grill to high heat or heat a grill pan on the stovetop.

2. **Shape the Burger Patties:** Divide the ground beef into four equal portions. Gently shape each portion into a patty, about 1 inch thick. Season both sides of each patty with salt and black pepper.

3. **Grill the Patties:** Place the burger patties on the hot grill or grill pan. Cook for about 3-4 minutes per side for medium-rare, or adjust the cooking time to your desired level of doneness. During the last minute of cooking, add a slice of cheese to each patty, and cover the grill or pan to allow the cheese to melt.

4. **Toast the Buns:** While the patties are cooking, split the hamburger buns and lightly toast them on the grill or in a toaster until they're slightly crispy.

5. **Assemble the Cheeseburgers:** Start by placing a lettuce leaf on the bottom half of each bun, followed by a tomato slice, red onion slices, and pickles if desired. Place a cheese-covered patty on top.

6. **Add Condiments:** Squeeze ketchup and mustard on the patty or use your preferred condiments.

7. **Complete the Cheeseburger:** Top with the other half of the bun.

8. **Serve:** Serve the cheeseburgers immediately with your choice of side dishes, such as french fries or coleslaw.

Enjoy your delicious homemade cheeseburgers! You can customize them by adding bacon, sautéed mushrooms, or other favorite toppings to suit your taste.

Hot Dog

Ingredients:

For the Hot Dogs:

- 4 hot dog sausages

- 4 hot dog buns

For the Toppings (You can choose your favorites):

- Ketchup

- Mustard

- Relish

- Chopped onions

- Sauerkraut

- Pickles

- Shredded cheese

- Jalapeño slices (for a spicy kick)

Instructions:

1. **Cook the Hot Dogs:**

   - There are various ways to cook hot dog sausages. You can grill them, pan-fry them, boil them, or even microwave them. Choose your preferred method.

2. **Grill Method:**

   - Preheat your grill to medium-high heat.

   - Place the hot dog sausages on the grill grates.

   - Grill for about 5-7 minutes, turning occasionally until they are heated through and have grill marks.

3. **Pan-Fry Method:**

   - Heat a skillet or frying pan over medium heat.

   - Place the hot dog sausages in the pan.

   - Cook for about 5-7 minutes, turning occasionally until they are heated through and browned.

4. **Boil Method:**

   - Bring a pot of water to a boil.

   - Carefully add the hot dog sausages.

- Boil for about 4-5 minutes until they are heated through.

5. **Microwave Method:**

   - Place the hot dog sausages on a microwave-safe plate.

   - Heat on high for 1-2 minutes until they are heated through.

6. **Prepare the Buns:**

   - While the hot dogs are cooking, split the hot dog buns, but don't separate them completely.

   - Optionally, you can lightly toast the buns in a toaster or on the grill for extra flavor and texture.

7. **Assemble the Hot Dogs:**

   - Place a cooked hot dog sausage in each bun.

8. **Add Toppings:**

   - Add your choice of toppings and condiments. Common options include ketchup, mustard, relish, chopped onions, sauerkraut, pickles, shredded cheese, and jalapeño slices.

9. **Serve:** Serve the hot dogs immediately while they're still warm and the buns are soft.

Enjoy your homemade hot dogs with your favorite toppings! You can customize them to suit your taste by adding any toppings you like.

French Fries

Ingredients:

- 4 large russet potatoes
- Vegetable oil for frying
- Salt, to taste

Instructions:

1. **Preheat the Oil:**

   - Pour enough vegetable oil into a deep fryer or a large, deep, heavy-bottomed pot to submerge the fries completely. Heat the oil to 350-375°F (175-190°C).

2. **Prepare the Potatoes:**

   - Wash the potatoes thoroughly to remove dirt. You can peel them if you prefer, but leaving the skin on can add extra flavor and texture.

   - Cut the potatoes into even-sized matchsticks or thin strips, about 1/4 to 1/2 inch thick. You can use a sharp knife or a French fry cutter for this.

3. **Rinse and Dry:**

   - Rinse the potato strips under cold water to remove excess starch.

   - Pat them dry with paper towels or a clean kitchen towel.

4. **First Fry (Blanching):**

   - Carefully add a handful of the potato strips to the hot oil. Be cautious not to overcrowd the fryer or pot.

   - Fry for about 3-4 minutes until they are pale and just starting to turn golden.

   - Remove with a slotted spoon or tongs and place them on a plate lined with paper towels to drain.

5. **Second Fry (Crisping):**

   - Once all the potatoes have been blanched, increase the oil temperature to 375-400°F (190-205°C).

   - Fry the potato strips in small batches again for about 2-3 minutes or until they turn golden brown and crispy.

   - Remove with a slotted spoon and place them on a fresh plate lined with paper towels.

6. **Season and Serve:**

   - Immediately after frying, season the French fries with salt while they're still hot.

- Serve them hot with your favorite condiments, such as ketchup, mayonnaise, or vinegar.

Enjoy your homemade crispy French fries! You can customize them with various seasonings like paprika, garlic powder, or grated Parmesan cheese for added flavor.

Buffalo Wings

Ingredients:

For the Wings:

- 2 pounds (about 900g) chicken wings, separated into drumettes and flats

- 1 cup all-purpose flour

- Salt and pepper, to taste

- Vegetable oil, for frying

For the Buffalo Sauce:

- 1/2 cup hot sauce (such as Frank's RedHot)

- 1/2 cup unsalted butter

- 1 tablespoon white vinegar

- 1/4 teaspoon cayenne pepper (adjust to taste)

- 1/4 teaspoon garlic powder

- Salt, to taste

For Serving:

- Celery sticks

- Carrot sticks

- Blue cheese dressing or ranch dressing

Instructions:

1. **Preheat the Oil:**

   - Pour enough vegetable oil into a deep fryer or a large, deep, heavy-bottomed pot to submerge the chicken wings. Heat the oil to 375°F (190°C).

2. **Prepare the Chicken Wings:**

   - In a bowl, mix the flour with a pinch of salt and pepper.

   - Dredge each chicken wing in the flour mixture, shaking off any excess.

3. **Fry the Chicken Wings:**

   - Carefully place the coated chicken wings in the hot oil. Be cautious not to overcrowd the fryer or pot.

   - Fry for about 10-12 minutes, or until the wings are golden brown and crispy.

4. **Make the Buffalo Sauce:**

   - While the wings are frying, melt the butter in a saucepan over low heat.

- Stir in the hot sauce, white vinegar, cayenne pepper, garlic powder, and a pinch of salt. Cook and stir until everything is well combined and heated through. Adjust the heat level to your preference by adding more or less cayenne pepper.

5. **Coat the Wings:**

   - Once the wings are done frying, use a slotted spoon to remove them from the oil and drain on a plate lined with paper towels.

   - While the wings are still hot, toss them in the Buffalo sauce until they are evenly coated.

6. **Serve:**

   - Arrange the Buffalo wings on a serving platter.

   - Serve with celery and carrot sticks on the side, along with blue cheese dressing or ranch dressing for dipping.

Enjoy your homemade Buffalo Wings! These spicy, tangy, and crispy wings are perfect for game days or as a tasty snack.

Philly Cheesesteak

Ingredients:

For the Steak Filling:

- 1 pound (450g) thinly sliced beef ribeye or sirloin

- 2 tablespoons vegetable oil

- 1 large onion, thinly sliced

- 1 large green bell pepper, thinly sliced

- Salt and black pepper, to taste

- 4 slices of provolone cheese (or American cheese)

- 4 hoagie rolls or sub rolls

Instructions:

1. **Preheat a Griddle or Skillet:**

   - Heat a griddle or large skillet over medium-high heat.

2. **Cook the Onions and Peppers:**

   - Add one tablespoon of vegetable oil to the hot skillet.

   - Add the thinly sliced onions and green bell peppers to the skillet.

   - Sauté them for about 5-7 minutes, stirring occasionally, until they become soft and slightly caramelized. Remove them from the skillet and set aside.

3. **Cook the Steak:**

   - Add the remaining tablespoon of vegetable oil to the skillet.

   - Place the thinly sliced beef in the skillet, spreading it out into an even layer.

   - Season the beef with salt and black pepper.

   - Cook for about 2-3 minutes, stirring occasionally, until the beef is browned and cooked through.

4. **Combine the Steak and Vegetables:**

   - Return the sautéed onions and peppers to the skillet with the cooked beef. Mix everything together and cook for another 1-2 minutes to heat through.

5. **Melt the Cheese:**

   - Divide the beef, onion, and pepper mixture into four portions in the skillet.

   - Place a slice of provolone cheese (or American cheese) over each portion.

- Cover the skillet with a lid or foil and let it cook for about 1 minute until the cheese is melted and gooey.

6. **Assemble the Philly Cheesesteak:**

   - Split the hoagie rolls or sub rolls lengthwise without cutting all the way through.

   - Using a spatula, carefully transfer each cheesy portion of the beef and vegetables onto a roll.

7. **Serve:**

   - Serve the Philly Cheesesteak sandwiches hot.

Enjoy your homemade Philly Cheesesteak sandwiches! They're delicious and full of savory flavor. You can also customize them with toppings like mushrooms, hot peppers, or mayonnaise, according to your preferences.

Poutine (Canada)

Ingredients:

- 4 cups frozen french fries or freshly cut potatoes (for a homemade touch)

- 2 cups cheese curds (preferably white cheddar cheese curds)

- 1 cup beef gravy (homemade or store-bought)

- Salt and black pepper, to taste

Instructions:

1. **Prepare the French Fries:**

   - If using frozen french fries, follow the package instructions to cook them until they are crispy and golden brown. If making fresh-cut fries from potatoes, follow these steps:

     - Peel and cut the potatoes into thin strips or your desired fry shape.

     - Rinse the potato strips in cold water to remove excess starch.

     - Pat them dry with paper towels.

     - Heat vegetable oil in a deep fryer or large, deep pot to 350-375°F (175-190°C).

     - Fry the potato strips in batches until they are golden brown and crispy, about 3-4 minutes per batch.

     - Remove them with a slotted spoon and place them on a plate lined with paper towels to drain. Season with salt while they're hot.

2. **Heat the Gravy:**

   - Warm the beef gravy in a saucepan over medium-low heat. Keep it warm until you're ready to use it.

3. **Assemble the Poutine:**

   - Place a portion of the cooked french fries on a serving plate or in a shallow bowl.

   - Sprinkle a generous amount of cheese curds over the hot fries. The cheese should start to melt slightly from the heat of the fries.

4. **Pour the Gravy:**

   - Pour the hot beef gravy over the fries and cheese curds, ensuring that it covers them evenly.

5. **Serve Immediately:**

   - Serve the Poutine immediately while it's hot and the cheese is melting into the gravy.

6. **Enjoy:**

- Use a fork or a fork and knife to dig in and enjoy the delicious combination of crispy fries, melty cheese curds, and savory gravy.

Poutine is a comforting and indulgent Canadian specialty. You can customize it by adding toppings like pulled pork, sautéed mushrooms, or caramelized onions if you'd like to create your own unique version.

Empanadas

Ingredients:

For the Dough:

- 2 1/2 cups all-purpose flour
- 1/2 teaspoon salt
- 1/2 cup (1 stick) cold unsalted butter, cut into small pieces
- 1/2 cup cold water
- 1 egg, beaten (for egg wash)

For the Filling:

- 1 pound (450g) ground beef or your choice of filling (e.g., chicken, cheese, vegetables)
- 1 medium onion, finely chopped
- 1 bell pepper, finely chopped (optional)
- 2 cloves garlic, minced
- 1/2 teaspoon ground cumin
- 1/2 teaspoon paprika
- Salt and black pepper, to taste
- 1/2 cup pitted green olives, sliced
- 2 hard-boiled eggs, chopped (optional)
- Vegetable oil, for frying

Instructions:

For the Dough:

1. **Prepare the Dough:**

    - In a large mixing bowl, combine the flour and salt.
    - Add the cold, diced butter and use a pastry cutter or your fingers to cut it into the flour until the mixture resembles coarse crumbs.

2. **Add Water:**

    - Gradually add cold water and mix until the dough comes together. You may need to use your hands to knead it gently.

3. **Chill the Dough:**

    - Form the dough into a ball, wrap it in plastic wrap, and refrigerate it for at least 30 minutes or until it's firm.

For the Filling:

4. **Prepare the Filling:**

    - In a skillet, heat a bit of oil over medium heat.

    - Add the finely chopped onion and bell pepper (if using) and sauté until they are soft and translucent.

    - Add the minced garlic and ground beef (or your chosen filling) and cook until the meat is browned and cooked through.

    - Season with ground cumin, paprika, salt, and black pepper.

    - Stir in the sliced green olives and chopped hard-boiled eggs (if using). Remove from heat.

Assemble the Empanadas:

5. **Roll Out the Dough:**

    - On a floured surface, roll out the chilled dough into a thin sheet, about 1/8 inch thick.

6. **Cut Out Circles:**

    - Use a round cutter (about 4-5 inches in diameter) to cut out circles from the dough.

7. **Fill and Fold:**

    - Place a spoonful of the meat filling onto the center of each dough circle.

    - Fold the dough over to create a half-moon shape and seal the edges by pressing with a fork or twisting them to create a decorative edge.

8. **Repeat:**

    - Continue filling, folding, and sealing until all the dough circles are used.

Frying the Empanadas:

9. **Heat the Oil:**

    - In a deep skillet or frying pan, heat enough vegetable oil for deep frying to 350°F (175°C).

10. **Fry the Empanadas:**

    - Carefully add the empanadas to the hot oil, a few at a time, making sure not to overcrowd the pan.

    - Fry until they are golden brown and crispy, about 3-4 minutes per side.

11. **Drain and Serve:**

    - Use a slotted spoon to remove the fried empanadas and place them on a plate lined with paper towels to drain any excess oil.

12. **Serve Hot:**

- Serve the empanadas hot and enjoy!

Empanadas are delicious when served fresh and warm. They can be a great appetizer or a main course, and you can customize the fillings to suit your taste.

Arepas (Venezuela)

Ingredients:

For the Arepa Dough:

- 2 cups pre-cooked cornmeal (such as Harina P.A.N. or Masarepa)
- 2 1/2 cups warm water
- 1 teaspoon salt
- 2 tablespoons vegetable oil (optional)

For the Arepa Filling (Optional, choose your favorite):

- Shredded beef
- Shredded chicken
- Black beans
- Cheese (queso fresco, mozzarella, or your choice)
- Avocado slices
- Salsa
- Sliced tomatoes
- Sliced onions
- Lettuce
- Mayonnaise

Instructions:

For the Arepa Dough:

1. **Mix the Ingredients:**

   - In a mixing bowl, combine the pre-cooked cornmeal and salt.
   - Gradually add the warm water while stirring continuously. Mix until the dough is smooth and free of lumps. It should have a playdough-like consistency.
   - If desired, add the vegetable oil and knead it into the dough until fully incorporated.

2. **Rest the Dough:**

   - Let the dough rest for about 5-10 minutes to allow the cornmeal to fully hydrate.

3. **Form Arepas:**

   - Take a portion of the dough and shape it into a ball, then flatten it into a round disc, about 1/2 to 3/4 inch thick. Arepas are typically about 4-5 inches in diameter, but you can make them smaller or larger according to your preference.

4. **Cook Arepas:**

- Heat a griddle or skillet over medium-high heat. Brush it lightly with oil or use a non-stick surface.

- Place the formed arepas on the hot griddle and cook for about 5-7 minutes on each side, or until they develop a golden-brown crust. They should sound hollow when tapped.

5. **Finish Cooking:**

- Once the arepas have a crispy exterior, transfer them to a preheated oven at 350°F (175°C) and bake for about 10-15 minutes to ensure they are fully cooked on the inside. Alternatively, you can continue cooking on the griddle, but baking helps to ensure they are thoroughly cooked.

For the Arepa Filling:

6. **Slice and Fill Arepas:**

- Carefully slice each arepa in half horizontally, creating a pocket inside.

- Fill the arepas with your choice of fillings. Common options include shredded beef, shredded chicken, black beans, cheese, avocado, salsa, tomatoes, onions, lettuce, and mayonnaise.

7. **Serve:**

- Serve the filled arepas while they're warm and enjoy!

Arepas are versatile and can be filled with a wide variety of ingredients. You can mix and match fillings to suit your taste. They make a delicious and satisfying meal or snack.

Ceviche (Peru)

Ingredients:

- 1 pound (450g) fresh white fish (such as tilapia, sea bass, or flounder), cut into small cubes
- 1/2 cup freshly squeezed lime juice (about 8-10 limes)
- 1/2 cup freshly squeezed lemon juice (about 2-3 lemons)
- 1 small red onion, thinly sliced
- 1-2 fresh hot chili peppers (aji amarillo or jalapeño), thinly sliced (adjust to your preferred level of spiciness)
- 1-2 cloves garlic, minced
- 1 teaspoon salt
- Freshly ground black pepper, to taste
- 1-2 tablespoons chopped fresh cilantro
- 1-2 tablespoons chopped fresh parsley
- Corn kernels (optional)
- Sweet potato, boiled and sliced (optional)
- Lettuce leaves (for serving)

Instructions:

1. **Prepare the Fish:**
   - Place the cubed fish in a glass or ceramic bowl. Ensure the fish is cut into small, uniform pieces for even marination.

2. **Marinate the Fish:**
   - Pour the freshly squeezed lime and lemon juice over the fish. The acid from the citrus juices will "cook" the fish. Make sure all the fish pieces are submerged in the juice.
   - Cover the bowl with plastic wrap or a lid and refrigerate. Allow the fish to marinate for at least 15-20 minutes or until the fish turns opaque and "cooked" (it should no longer be translucent).

3. **Prepare the Vegetables:**
   - While the fish is marinating, thinly slice the red onion, chili peppers, and mince the garlic.
   - If you prefer a milder ceviche, you can remove the seeds and membranes from the chili peppers.

4. **Combine Ingredients:**

- Drain the excess citrus juice from the fish.
- Add the sliced red onions, chili peppers, minced garlic, salt, and black pepper to the marinated fish. Mix gently to combine.

5. **Add Fresh Herbs:**

- Stir in the chopped fresh cilantro and parsley. These herbs will add a burst of fresh flavor to your ceviche.

6. **Optional Ingredients:**

- If desired, you can add cooked corn kernels to the ceviche for additional texture and sweetness. Additionally, serve the ceviche with slices of boiled sweet potato for a traditional accompaniment.

7. **Serve:**

- To serve, arrange lettuce leaves on plates or in a bowl.
- Spoon the ceviche mixture onto the lettuce leaves.
- Garnish with additional fresh cilantro and parsley if desired.

8. **Enjoy:**

- Serve your Peruvian ceviche immediately while it's fresh and flavorful.

Ceviche is a delightful and refreshing dish that's perfect for a light and zesty appetizer or a main course. It's important to use fresh and high-quality fish for the best results, and feel free to adjust the level of spiciness to your liking by adding more or fewer chili peppers.

Tamales (Mexico)

Ingredients:

For the Tamale Dough (Masa):

- 2 cups masa harina (corn masa flour)
- 1 1/2 cups chicken or vegetable broth (warm)
- 2/3 cup lard or vegetable shortening
- 1 teaspoon baking powder
- 1 teaspoon salt
- 1/2 teaspoon ground cumin (optional)

For the Filling (Choose one or create your own):

- Shredded chicken, beef, or pork
- Cheese (queso fresco or your choice)
- Roasted vegetables
- Salsa
- Refried beans

For the Corn Husks:

- Dried corn husks, soaked in warm water until pliable

Instructions:

Prepare the Corn Husks:

1. Place the dried corn husks in a large bowl or basin filled with warm water. Allow them to soak for at least 30 minutes or until they become pliable. You may need to weigh them down with a plate to keep them submerged.

Prepare the Tamale Dough (Masa):

2. In a mixing bowl, combine the masa harina, baking powder, salt, and ground cumin (if using).

3. In a separate bowl, beat the lard or vegetable shortening until it becomes fluffy, about 1-2 minutes.

4. Gradually add the masa harina mixture to the beaten lard, alternating with the warm chicken or vegetable broth. Mix until the dough is smooth and has a consistency similar to thick cake batter.

Assemble the Tamales:

5. Take a soaked corn husk and shake off any excess water. Place it on a clean surface with the wide end facing you.

6. Spread a spoonful of the tamale dough onto the center of the corn husk, leaving about 1-2 inches on the sides and at the top and bottom.

7. Add your choice of filling on top of the masa. You can use shredded chicken, beef, pork, cheese, roasted vegetables, salsa, or refried beans, depending on your preference.

8. Fold the sides of the corn husk over the filling, then fold up the bottom to enclose the tamale. The top should remain open.

9. Repeat the process with the remaining corn husks, masa, and filling.

Cook the Tamales:

10. Place a steamer basket in a large pot and add enough water to reach just below the steamer. Make sure the water doesn't touch the tamales when they're placed in the steamer.

11. Stand the tamales upright, open side up, in the steamer basket. You can use extra corn husks to line the bottom of the basket to prevent sticking.

12. Cover the tamales with more soaked corn husks and a damp kitchen towel or foil.

13. Steam the tamales over medium heat for about 1.5 to 2 hours, or until the masa is firm and easily separates from the corn husks.

Serve the Tamales:

14. Allow the tamales to cool slightly before serving. They are typically served with salsa or your choice of toppings.

Enjoy your homemade tamales, a delicious and traditional Mexican treat!

Fish and Chips (UK)

Ingredients:

For the Fish:

- 4 fillets of white fish (such as cod, haddock, or pollock), about 6-8 ounces each

- Salt and freshly ground black pepper

- 1 cup all-purpose flour, for dredging

- 2 large eggs

- 1 cup breadcrumbs (preferably panko breadcrumbs)

- Vegetable oil, for frying

For the Chips (Fries):

- 4 large russet potatoes, peeled and cut into thick strips

- Vegetable oil, for frying

- Salt, to taste

For Serving:

- Malt vinegar

- Tartar sauce

- Peas or mushy peas (optional)

Instructions:

For the Fish:

1. **Prepare the Fish Fillets:**

    - Pat the fish fillets dry with paper towels.

    - Season them with salt and freshly ground black pepper.

2. **Dredge the Fish:**

    - Dredge each fish fillet in the all-purpose flour, shaking off any excess.

    - Dip the floured fillets into beaten eggs.

    - Coat them evenly with breadcrumbs, pressing the breadcrumbs onto the fish to adhere.

3. **Heat the Oil:**

    - In a deep fryer or large, deep, heavy-bottomed pot, heat vegetable oil to 350-375°F (175-190°C).

4. **Fry the Fish:**

- Carefully add the breaded fish fillets to the hot oil. Fry for about 5-7 minutes, turning once, until the fish is golden brown and cooked through. The cooking time may vary depending on the thickness of the fillets. Ensure they are cooked to an internal temperature of 145°F (63°C).

5. **Drain and Keep Warm:**

   - Use a slotted spoon or wire rack to remove the fried fish from the oil and place them on a plate lined with paper towels to drain. Keep the fish warm in a preheated oven at a low temperature.

For the Chips (Fries):

6. **Prepare the Chips:**

   - Heat vegetable oil in a deep fryer or a large, deep pot to 325-350°F (160-175°C).

   - Carefully add the cut potato strips in batches to the hot oil.

   - Fry for about 3-4 minutes, or until they are just starting to become tender but not yet browned.

   - Remove the partially cooked chips with a slotted spoon and drain them on paper towels.

7. **Final Fry:**

   - Increase the oil temperature to 375-400°F (190-205°C).

   - Return the partially cooked chips to the hot oil in batches and fry for an additional 2-3 minutes or until they are golden brown and crispy.

   - Remove the chips from the oil, drain on paper towels, and immediately sprinkle with salt.

Serve Fish and Chips:

8. **Serve Hot:**

   - Serve the hot, crispy fish and chips with malt vinegar and tartar sauce on the side.

   - Optionally, serve with peas or mushy peas for a traditional British touch.

Enjoy your homemade Fish and Chips, a classic British comfort food!

Croissant Sandwich (France)

Ingredients:

For the Croissants:

- 4 large croissants (freshly baked or store-bought)
- 4 slices of ham or smoked salmon (or your preferred protein)
- 4 slices of Swiss cheese (or your preferred cheese)
- Butter, for spreading (optional)

For the Filling (Customize to Your Liking):

- Lettuce leaves
- Sliced tomatoes
- Sliced cucumbers
- Sliced red onions
- Avocado slices
- Dijon mustard or mayonnaise (optional)
- Fresh herbs (such as basil or parsley, optional)

Instructions:

1. **Prepare the Croissants:**
   - If using freshly baked croissants, allow them to cool slightly before handling.
   - If the croissants are not pre-sliced, carefully slice them horizontally, creating a top and bottom half for each croissant.

2. **Layer the Filling:**
   - Start by spreading a thin layer of butter, Dijon mustard, or mayonnaise on the inside of the croissants (optional).

3. **Add Protein:**
   - Place a slice of ham, smoked salmon, or your preferred protein on the bottom half of each croissant.

4. **Add Cheese:**
   - Layer a slice of Swiss cheese or your chosen cheese on top of the protein.

5. **Add Vegetables and Herbs:**
   - Add lettuce leaves, sliced tomatoes, cucumbers, red onions, avocado slices, and fresh herbs to your liking. You can mix and match these according to your preference.

6. **Assemble the Sandwich:**

   - Place the top half of the croissant on the layered ingredients to create a sandwich.

7. **Serve:**

   - Serve your croissant sandwiches immediately, either whole or cut in half for easier handling.

Croissant sandwiches are wonderfully versatile, and you can customize them with your favorite ingredients. They are perfect for a light breakfast, brunch, or lunch. Enjoy the combination of flaky croissants with savory fillings and fresh vegetables for a delightful French-inspired meal.

Gyros (Greece)

Ingredients:

For the Gyros Meat:

- 1.5 pounds (680g) boneless lamb, beef, or chicken (a mixture of lamb and beef is traditional)
- 2 cloves garlic, minced
- 1 teaspoon dried oregano
- 1 teaspoon ground cumin
- 1 teaspoon paprika
- Salt and black pepper, to taste
- 2 tablespoons olive oil

For the Tzatziki Sauce:

- 1 cup Greek yogurt
- 1 cucumber, grated and drained
- 2 cloves garlic, minced
- 1 tablespoon fresh lemon juice
- 1 tablespoon fresh dill, chopped (or 1 teaspoon dried dill)
- Salt and black pepper, to taste

For Assembling:

- Pita bread or flatbreads
- Sliced tomatoes
- Sliced red onions
- Sliced cucumbers
- Lettuce leaves
- Kalamata olives (optional)
- Feta cheese (optional)

Instructions:

For the Gyros Meat:

1. **Prepare the Meat:**
    - If using chicken, thinly slice it into strips. If using lamb or beef, thinly slice it against the grain.

- In a bowl, combine the minced garlic, dried oregano, ground cumin, paprika, salt, black pepper, and olive oil.

2. **Marinate the Meat:**

   - Add the sliced meat to the marinade, ensuring it's well coated.

   - Cover and refrigerate for at least 30 minutes, or ideally, marinate it overnight for the best flavor.

3. **Cook the Meat:**

   - Heat a grill or a skillet over medium-high heat.

   - Thread the marinated meat onto skewers if you're using lamb or beef.

   - Grill or cook the meat for about 3-5 minutes per side, or until it's cooked through and slightly charred.

4. **Slice the Cooked Meat:**

   - Once cooked, remove the meat from the skewers and thinly slice it.

For the Tzatziki Sauce:

5. **Prepare the Tzatziki:**

   - In a bowl, combine the Greek yogurt, grated and drained cucumber, minced garlic, fresh lemon juice, fresh dill, salt, and black pepper.

   - Mix well and refrigerate until you're ready to serve.

Assemble the Gyros:

6. **Warm the Pita Bread:**

   - Warm the pita bread or flatbreads in a skillet or microwave for a few seconds.

7. **Layer the Ingredients:**

   - Place a lettuce leaf on each pita.

   - Add slices of the grilled meat.

   - Top with sliced tomatoes, red onions, cucumbers, Kalamata olives (if using), and crumbled feta cheese (if using).

8. **Drizzle with Tzatziki:**

   - Drizzle a generous amount of tzatziki sauce over the gyro.

9. **Fold and Serve:**

   - Fold the pita over the ingredients to create a gyro sandwich.

10. **Serve:**

   - Serve your delicious gyro sandwiches immediately.

Italian Gelato

Ingredients:

- 2 cups whole milk

- 1 cup heavy cream

- 3/4 cup granulated sugar

- 1 vanilla bean or 1 tablespoon pure vanilla extract

- 4 large egg yolks

- Flavors and mix-ins of your choice (chocolate chips, fruit puree, nuts, etc.)

Instructions:

1. **Prepare the Base:**

   - In a medium saucepan, combine the whole milk and heavy cream. Heat over medium-low heat until it's warm but not boiling. Remove from heat.

2. **Prepare the Vanilla Bean (if using):**

   - If using a vanilla bean, split it lengthwise and scrape out the seeds using the back of a knife. Add both the seeds and the scraped vanilla bean pod to the milk mixture. If using vanilla extract, skip this step.

3. **Whisk Egg Yolks and Sugar:**

   - In a separate bowl, whisk together the egg yolks and granulated sugar until the mixture becomes pale and slightly thickened.

4. **Temper the Eggs:**

   - Gradually pour a small amount of the warm milk mixture into the egg yolk mixture, whisking constantly. This tempers the eggs, preventing them from curdling.

5. **Combine and Cook:**

   - Pour the tempered egg mixture back into the saucepan with the remaining milk mixture. If you used a vanilla bean, remove it now.

   - Cook the mixture over low heat, stirring constantly with a wooden spoon or silicone spatula until it thickens slightly. It should coat the back of the spoon and reach about 170°F (77°C). Do not let it boil.

6. **Strain and Cool:**

   - Remove the saucepan from the heat and strain the mixture through a fine-mesh sieve into a clean bowl. This step removes any bits of cooked egg or vanilla bean.

   - Allow the mixture to cool to room temperature.

7. **Add Vanilla Extract (if using):**

- If you didn't use a vanilla bean, add the vanilla extract to the cooled mixture and stir to combine.

8. **Chill the Mixture:**

   - Cover the bowl with plastic wrap, ensuring it touches the surface of the mixture to prevent a skin from forming.

   - Refrigerate for at least 4 hours or, preferably, overnight to chill thoroughly.

9. **Churn the Gelato:**

   - Pour the chilled mixture into an ice cream maker and churn according to the manufacturer's instructions. This usually takes about 20-30 minutes.

10. **Add Mix-Ins (if desired):**

    - In the last few minutes of churning, add any desired mix-ins, such as chocolate chips or fruit puree. Let the ice cream maker incorporate them evenly.

11. **Transfer and Freeze:**

    - Transfer the churned gelato to an airtight container and freeze for an additional 2-3 hours or until it reaches your desired firmness.

12. **Serve:**

    - Scoop the Italian gelato into bowls or cones and enjoy!

Italian gelato is known for its rich and creamy texture. You can customize it with a wide variety of flavors and mix-ins to create your own unique gelato experience. Buon appetito!

S u s h i (J a p a n)

Making sushi at home can be a fun and rewarding culinary adventure. Here's a basic recipe for making sushi rolls, also known as Maki Sushi. Traditional sushi also includes Nigiri (hand-pressed sushi) and Sashimi (thinly sliced raw fish), but let's start with sushi rolls:

Ingredients:

For the Sushi Rice:

- 1 cup sushi rice

- 2 cups water

- 1/4 cup rice vinegar

- 2 tablespoons sugar

- 1 teaspoon salt

For the Sushi Fillings (Choose your favorites):

- Fresh fish (such as tuna, salmon, or shrimp), thinly sliced

- Vegetables (such as cucumber, avocado, and carrot), thinly sliced into strips

- Nori seaweed sheets

- Soy sauce, pickled ginger, and wasabi (for serving)

Equipment:

- Bamboo sushi rolling mat (makisu)

- Plastic wrap or a gallon-sized resealable bag

- Sharp knife

- A bowl of water with a bit of rice vinegar (for dipping your fingers)

Instructions:

For the Sushi Rice:

1. **Rinse and Cook the Rice:**

    - Rinse the sushi rice in a fine-mesh strainer until the water runs clear.

    - Combine the rinsed rice and water in a saucepan. Bring it to a boil, then reduce the heat to low, cover, and simmer for about 15 minutes or until the rice is tender and the water is absorbed.

    - Remove the cooked rice from the heat and let it sit, covered, for 10 minutes.

2. **Prepare the Sushi Vinegar:**

    - In a small saucepan, heat the rice vinegar, sugar, and salt over low heat until the sugar and salt dissolve. Remove from heat and let it cool.

3. **Season the Rice:**

- Transfer the cooked rice to a large wooden or glass bowl.

- Drizzle the sushi vinegar mixture over the rice and gently fold it in using a wooden spatula or a rice paddle while fanning the rice to cool it quickly. Continue until the rice reaches room temperature.

For Assembling the Sushi Rolls:

4. **Prepare Your Workstation:**

- Place the bamboo sushi rolling mat on a clean surface.

- Lay a sheet of plastic wrap or a resealable bag on top of the mat.

5. **Lay Out a Nori Sheet:**

- Lay a sheet of nori, shiny side down, on top of the plastic wrap.

6. **Moisten Your Fingers:**

- Dip your fingers in the bowl of water with a bit of rice vinegar to prevent the rice from sticking to your hands.

7. **Spread the Sushi Rice:**

- Take a handful of sushi rice and spread it evenly over the nori sheet, leaving a small border at the top.

8. **Add Fillings:**

- Place your choice of fillings (fish, vegetables, etc.) in the center of the rice.

9. **Roll the Sushi:**

- Lift the bamboo mat's edge closest to you, starting the roll.

- Roll the nori and rice tightly over the fillings, using the bamboo mat to help shape the roll.

- Wet the top border of the nori sheet and press it to seal the roll.

10. **Slice the Roll:**

- Use a sharp knife dipped in water to slice the roll into bite-sized pieces.

11. **Repeat:**

- Repeat the process with the remaining nori sheets and fillings.

12. **Serve and Enjoy:**

- Serve your homemade sushi rolls with soy sauce, pickled ginger, and wasabi.

Sushi-making can take a bit of practice, especially rolling it neatly, but it's a rewarding and enjoyable process. Customize your sushi with your favorite ingredients and enjoy the delicious results!

R a m e n   (J a p a n)

Making homemade ramen is a flavorful and comforting culinary experience. Here's a basic recipe for a delicious bowl of Japanese Ramen:

Ingredients:

For the Broth:

- 8 cups chicken or vegetable broth (homemade or store-bought)
- 2 cloves garlic, minced
- 1 thumb-sized piece of ginger, sliced
- 2-3 green onions, chopped
- 1-2 tablespoons soy sauce (adjust to taste)
- 1-2 teaspoons miso paste (adjust to taste)
- 1-2 teaspoons sesame oil (adjust to taste)
- Salt and pepper, to taste

For the Ramen Bowl:

- 8 ounces ramen noodles
- Sliced cooked chicken, pork, or tofu (optional)
- Soft-boiled eggs, halved
- Sliced bamboo shoots (menma)
- Nori seaweed sheets, cut into strips
- Corn kernels (optional)
- Bean sprouts (optional)
- Sliced green onions (optional)
- Sesame seeds (optional)

Instructions:

For the Broth:

1. **Prepare the Aromatics:**

    - In a large pot, heat a bit of vegetable oil over medium heat.
    - Add minced garlic, sliced ginger, and chopped green onions. Sauté for a few minutes until fragrant.

2. **Simmer the Broth:**

   - Pour in the chicken or vegetable broth and bring it to a boil.

   - Reduce the heat to a gentle simmer and let it cook for about 20-30 minutes to infuse the flavors.

3. **Season the Broth:**

   - Add soy sauce, miso paste, and sesame oil to the broth. Adjust the quantities to taste. Miso paste can be quite salty, so be cautious and add it gradually.

4. **Taste and Adjust:**

   - Taste the broth and adjust the seasoning with salt and pepper as needed. Keep it warm on low heat.

For the Ramen Bowl:

5. **Cook the Ramen Noodles:**

   - Cook the ramen noodles according to the package instructions until they are al dente.

   - Drain and rinse them under cold water to stop the cooking process.

6. **Prepare Toppings:**

   - While the noodles are cooking, prepare your chosen toppings. You can use sliced cooked chicken, pork, or tofu, soft-boiled eggs, bamboo shoots, nori strips, corn kernels, bean sprouts, sliced green onions, and sesame seeds.

7. **Assemble the Ramen Bowl:**

   - Divide the cooked ramen noodles among serving bowls.

   - Ladle the hot broth over the noodles, ensuring they are submerged.

   - Arrange your desired toppings on top of the broth.

8. **Serve and Enjoy:**

   - Serve your homemade ramen hot and enjoy your delicious bowl of comfort food!

Feel free to customize your ramen bowl with your favorite ingredients and adjust the seasonings to your taste. Homemade ramen offers endless possibilities for creating your perfect bowl of Japanese comfort food.

Dim Sum (China)

Dim Sum is a delightful Chinese culinary tradition of small, flavorful dishes served with tea. While making all the dim sum varieties from scratch can be quite an undertaking, I'll provide a recipe for one of the most popular dim sum dishes, Shumai (Siu Mai), which are open-faced dumplings filled with seasoned pork and shrimp.

Ingredients:

For the Filling:

- 1/2 pound ground pork
- 1/2 pound shrimp, peeled, deveined, and finely chopped
- 2 cloves garlic, minced
- 1-inch piece of ginger, minced
- 2 green onions, finely chopped
- 1 tablespoon soy sauce
- 1 tablespoon oyster sauce
- 1 teaspoon sesame oil
- 1 teaspoon sugar
- 1/2 teaspoon salt
- 1/4 teaspoon white pepper

For the Dumpling Wrappers:

- Store-bought round dumpling wrappers (usually about 3-inch in diameter)

For Garnish:

- Pea shoots, cilantro leaves, or sliced green onions (optional)
- Soy sauce or chili oil (for dipping)

Instructions:

Prepare the Filling:

1. In a large bowl, combine the ground pork, chopped shrimp, minced garlic, minced ginger, chopped green onions, soy sauce, oyster sauce, sesame oil, sugar, salt, and white pepper.
2. Mix the filling ingredients together thoroughly until well combined.

Assemble the Shumai:

3. Take a dumpling wrapper and place it in the palm of your hand or on a clean work surface.

4. Spoon a small amount of the filling mixture (about a tablespoon) onto the center of the wrapper.

5. Gather the edges of the wrapper and gently pleat them around the filling, leaving the top open and exposed. The pleats should naturally form as you fold the wrapper.

6. Press the filling down slightly and tap the bottom of the dumpling on a flat surface to create a flat base so it can stand upright.

Steam the Shumai:

7. Place the assembled shumai on a parchment paper-lined steamer tray or bamboo steamer, leaving some space between them to prevent sticking.

8. Steam the shumai over boiling water for about 12-15 minutes, or until the filling is cooked through and the wrappers become slightly translucent.

Serve the Shumai:

9. Carefully remove the shumai from the steamer.

10. Garnish with pea shoots, cilantro leaves, or sliced green onions if desired.

11. Serve the shumai hot with soy sauce or chili oil for dipping.

Enjoy your homemade Shumai as part of your homemade dim sum spread. Dim Sum often consists of a variety of dishes, so you can explore other recipes like dumplings, buns, and spring rolls to create a complete dim sum experience at home.

Thai Green Curry

Thai Green Curry is a fragrant and delicious Thai dish known for its rich, aromatic flavors. Here's a recipe to make Thai Green Curry at home:

Ingredients:

For the Green Curry Paste:

- 2-3 green Thai chilies (adjust to your spice preference)
- 2-3 cloves garlic
- 1 shallot, chopped
- 1 stalk lemongrass, sliced (use the tender white part)
- 1 thumb-sized piece of galangal or ginger, sliced
- 1 teaspoon ground coriander
- 1/2 teaspoon ground cumin
- 1/2 teaspoon ground white pepper
- 1 teaspoon shrimp paste (optional, for authenticity)
- Zest from 1 lime
- 2-3 fresh kaffir lime leaves (optional, for extra aroma)
- Small bunch of fresh cilantro stems

For the Curry:

- 1 pound (450g) chicken, beef, shrimp, tofu, or vegetables (cut into bite-sized pieces)
- 2-3 tablespoons green curry paste (adjust to your spice preference)
- 1 can (14 oz or 400ml) coconut milk
- 1 cup vegetables (such as bamboo shoots, bell peppers, and Thai eggplant)
- 2-3 tablespoons fish sauce (or soy sauce for a vegetarian version)
- 1-2 tablespoons palm sugar or brown sugar
- Fresh Thai basil leaves or basil leaves (for garnish)
- Sliced red chili (for garnish, optional)

Instructions:

Prepare the Green Curry Paste:

1. In a mortar and pestle or a food processor, combine all the green curry paste ingredients. Pound or process them into a smooth and fragrant paste. You can add a little coconut milk to help with blending if needed.

Prepare the Curry:

2. Heat a large pan or wok over medium-high heat. Add a couple of tablespoons of the thick part of the coconut milk (from the top of the can) and stir in the green curry paste. Cook for a few minutes until fragrant, stirring constantly.

3. Add the protein of your choice (chicken, beef, shrimp, tofu, or vegetables) to the pan. Stir-fry for a few minutes until the meat is cooked or the tofu/vegetables are lightly browned.

4. Pour in the remaining coconut milk and bring the mixture to a gentle simmer.

5. Add the vegetables to the curry. Thai eggplants, bamboo shoots, and bell peppers are traditional choices, but you can use any vegetables you prefer.

6. Season the curry with fish sauce (or soy sauce for a vegetarian version) and palm sugar (or brown sugar) to taste. Start with 2-3 tablespoons of fish sauce and 1-2 tablespoons of sugar, and adjust according to your preferences for sweetness and saltiness.

7. Simmer the curry for about 10-15 minutes, or until the vegetables are tender and the flavors have melded together.

8. Taste and adjust the seasoning if needed.

9. Just before serving, stir in fresh Thai basil leaves or regular basil leaves for a burst of flavor.

Serve the Thai Green Curry:

10. Ladle the green curry into bowls and garnish with sliced red chili (for extra heat, if desired).

11. Serve the Thai Green Curry hot over steamed jasmine rice or noodles.

Enjoy your homemade Thai Green Curry, a flavorful and aromatic Thai classic!

Biryani (India)

Biryani is a beloved and flavorful Indian rice dish made with aromatic basmati rice, meat or vegetables, and a blend of fragrant spices. Here's a recipe for Chicken Biryani:

Ingredients:

For the Marinated Chicken:

- 2 pounds (about 900g) chicken, cut into pieces
- 1 cup yogurt
- 1 teaspoon ginger paste
- 1 teaspoon garlic paste
- 1/2 teaspoon turmeric powder
- 1 teaspoon red chili powder (adjust to your spice preference)
- 1 teaspoon garam masala
- Salt, to taste
- Juice of 1 lemon

For the Rice:

- 2 cups basmati rice, soaked for 30 minutes and drained
- 4-5 cups water
- 2-3 green cardamom pods
- 2-3 cloves
- 1-inch cinnamon stick
- 1 bay leaf
- Salt, to taste

For Assembling:

- 2-3 tablespoons vegetable oil or ghee (clarified butter)
- 2 onions, thinly sliced
- 2-3 green chilies, slit (adjust to your spice preference)
- 1/2 cup fresh cilantro leaves, chopped
- 1/2 cup fresh mint leaves, chopped
- Saffron strands soaked in 2 tablespoons warm milk (optional, for garnish)
- Ghee or melted butter (for garnish)

Instructions:

Marinate the Chicken:

1. In a large bowl, combine the chicken pieces with yogurt, ginger paste, garlic paste, turmeric powder, red chili powder, garam masala, salt, and lemon juice. Mix well to ensure the chicken is evenly coated with the marinade.

2. Cover the bowl and refrigerate for at least 2 hours or overnight for the best flavor.

Prepare the Rice:

3. In a large pot, bring 4-5 cups of water to a boil. Add the soaked and drained basmati rice.

4. Add the green cardamom pods, cloves, cinnamon stick, bay leaf, and salt to the boiling water.

5. Cook the rice until it's about 70-80% done. It should still have a slight bite. Drain the rice and set it aside.

Assemble the Biryani:

6. In a large heavy-bottomed pan or a biryani pot, heat vegetable oil or ghee over medium heat.

7. Add the thinly sliced onions and cook until they turn golden brown and crispy. Remove some of the fried onions and set them aside for garnish.

8. Add the marinated chicken to the pan along with the green chilies. Cook for about 10-15 minutes, stirring occasionally, until the chicken is cooked through and the spices are fragrant.

9. Layer the partially cooked rice over the cooked chicken. Sprinkle half of the chopped cilantro and mint leaves over the rice.

10. Drizzle saffron-soaked milk (if using) and a little ghee or melted butter over the rice.

11. Top with the remaining chopped cilantro and mint leaves.

Dum Cooking (Slow Cooking):

12. Cover the pan with a tight-fitting lid or seal it with aluminum foil to trap the steam.

13. Reduce the heat to low and let the biryani simmer for about 20-25 minutes. This slow cooking process allows the flavors to meld, and the rice and chicken to finish cooking together.

Serve the Chicken Biryani:

14. Carefully open the lid, and using a fork, gently fluff the biryani to mix the layers.

15. Garnish with the reserved fried onions.

16. Serve the chicken biryani hot with raita (yogurt sauce) or a side salad.

Enjoy your homemade Chicken Biryani, a flavorful and aromatic Indian classic!

Shawarma

Shawarma is a delicious Middle Eastern street food dish made with thinly sliced marinated meat (usually beef, chicken, lamb, or a combination) that's roasted on a vertical rotisserie. It's typically served in a flatbread like pita or laffa bread and topped with a variety of accompaniments and sauces. Here's a recipe for Chicken Shawarma:

Ingredients:

For the Marinade:

- 1.5 pounds (about 680g) boneless, skinless chicken thighs or chicken breast
- 3 cloves garlic, minced
- 1 teaspoon ground cumin
- 1 teaspoon ground coriander
- 1 teaspoon ground paprika
- 1/2 teaspoon ground turmeric
- 1/2 teaspoon ground cinnamon
- 1/4 teaspoon cayenne pepper (adjust to your spice preference)
- Salt and black pepper, to taste
- 3 tablespoons plain Greek yogurt
- Juice of 1 lemon
- 2 tablespoons olive oil

For the Shawarma Sauce (Tahini Sauce):

- 1/4 cup tahini (sesame paste)
- 2 tablespoons lemon juice
- 2 tablespoons water
- 1 clove garlic, minced
- 1/4 teaspoon ground cumin
- Salt and black pepper, to taste

For Serving:

- Pita bread or flatbreads
- Sliced tomatoes
- Sliced cucumbers
- Thinly sliced red onions

- Fresh parsley or cilantro leaves

- Hot sauce (optional)

Instructions:

Marinate the Chicken:

1. In a bowl, combine minced garlic, ground cumin, ground coriander, ground paprika, ground turmeric, ground cinnamon, cayenne pepper, salt, black pepper, Greek yogurt, lemon juice, and olive oil.

2. Add the chicken pieces to the marinade and coat them well. Cover and refrigerate for at least 1 hour, or overnight for the best flavor.

Cook the Chicken:

3. Preheat your grill or a skillet over medium-high heat.

4. Thread the marinated chicken pieces onto skewers if using a grill. If using a skillet, you can cook them directly in the pan.

5. Grill or cook the chicken for about 5-7 minutes per side or until it's cooked through and has a nice char. Cooking times may vary depending on the thickness of the chicken.

6. Remove the cooked chicken from the skewers or pan and let it rest for a few minutes.

Prepare the Shawarma Sauce (Tahini Sauce):

7. In a small bowl, whisk together tahini, lemon juice, water, minced garlic, ground cumin, salt, and black pepper until you have a smooth and creamy sauce. Adjust the consistency with more water if needed.

Assemble the Chicken Shawarma:

8. Warm the pita bread or flatbreads.

9. Lay out each pita bread or flatbread, and spread a generous spoonful of the tahini sauce on it.

10. Place slices of the cooked chicken on top of the sauce.

11. Add sliced tomatoes, cucumbers, red onions, and fresh parsley or cilantro leaves.

12. Optionally, drizzle some hot sauce over the toppings for extra heat.

13. Roll up the pita or flatbread, tucking in the sides as you go, to create a wrap.

14. Serve the Chicken Shawarma wraps immediately.

Enjoy your homemade Chicken Shawarma, a flavorful Middle Eastern treat! You can customize the toppings and sauces to suit your preferences.

Falafel

Falafel is a popular Middle Eastern dish made from ground chickpeas or fava beans, mixed with herbs and spices, shaped into balls or patties, and deep-fried until crispy. Here's a recipe for homemade falafel:

Ingredients:

For the Falafel Mixture:

- 1 1/2 cups dried chickpeas (or canned chickpeas, drained and rinsed)

- 1 small onion, roughly chopped

- 3-4 cloves garlic, minced

- 1/4 cup fresh parsley, chopped

- 1/4 cup fresh cilantro, chopped

- 1 teaspoon ground cumin

- 1 teaspoon ground coriander

- 1/4 teaspoon cayenne pepper (adjust to your spice preference)

- Salt and black pepper, to taste

- 1/2-1 teaspoon baking powder

- 4-6 tablespoons all-purpose flour

- Vegetable oil for frying

For Serving:

- Pita bread or flatbreads

- Tahini sauce or yogurt-based sauce

- Sliced cucumbers, tomatoes, and lettuce

- Sliced red onions

- Pickles or pickled vegetables

- Fresh herbs like parsley, mint, or cilantro

- Hot sauce or chili sauce (optional)

Instructions:

Prepare the Chickpeas:

1. If using dried chickpeas, rinse them thoroughly and soak in cold water for at least 12 hours or overnight. Drain well.

Make the Falafel Mixture:

2. In a food processor, combine the soaked and drained chickpeas, chopped onion, minced garlic, fresh parsley, fresh cilantro, ground cumin, ground coriander, cayenne pepper, salt, black pepper, and baking powder. Pulse until you have a coarse mixture with a uniform texture.

3. Transfer the mixture to a bowl and add 4 tablespoons of all-purpose flour. Mix well. The mixture should hold together when you press it into a ball. If it's too wet, add more flour, one tablespoon at a time, until it reaches the right consistency.

4. Cover the bowl and refrigerate the mixture for at least 1 hour. Chilling helps the mixture firm up and makes it easier to shape.

Shape and Fry the Falafel:

5. Heat vegetable oil in a deep pot or skillet to 350°F (175°C).

6. While the oil is heating, shape the falafel mixture into small balls or patties using your hands or a falafel scoop. You can make them about 1-1.5 inches in diameter.

7. Carefully place the shaped falafel into the hot oil and fry until they are deep golden brown and crispy, about 3-5 minutes per side. Fry in batches, making sure not to overcrowd the pan.

8. Use a slotted spoon to remove the falafel from the oil and place them on a plate lined with paper towels to drain any excess oil.

Serve the Falafel:

9. Serve the falafel in pita bread or flatbreads. You can split the bread and stuff it with falafel and your choice of toppings: tahini sauce, sliced cucumbers, tomatoes, lettuce, sliced red onions, pickles, fresh herbs, and hot sauce.

10. Enjoy your homemade falafel!

Falafel is a versatile dish that you can customize to your liking. Feel free to adjust the seasoning and toppings according to your preferences for a delicious Middle Eastern meal.

Hummus

Hummus is a creamy and flavorful Middle Eastern dip made primarily from cooked chickpeas, tahini (sesame paste), lemon juice, garlic, and olive oil. Here's a simple recipe for homemade hummus:

Ingredients:

- 1 1/2 cups cooked chickpeas (canned or cooked from dried chickpeas)

- 1/3 cup tahini

- 1/4 cup fresh lemon juice (about 1 large lemon)

- 2 cloves garlic, minced

- 2 tablespoons extra-virgin olive oil, plus more for garnish

- 1/2 teaspoon ground cumin

- Salt, to taste

- 2-3 tablespoons water, as needed

- Optional garnishes: paprika, chopped fresh parsley, pine nuts, or olives

Instructions:

Prepare the Chickpeas:

1. If using canned chickpeas, drain and rinse them thoroughly. If using dried chickpeas, cook them according to the package instructions until they are soft and tender. Be sure to drain them well.

Make the Hummus:

2. In a food processor, combine the cooked chickpeas, tahini, fresh lemon juice, minced garlic, olive oil, ground cumin, and a pinch of salt.

3. Process the mixture until it's smooth and creamy, stopping to scrape down the sides of the food processor as needed. If the hummus is too thick, add water, one tablespoon at a time, and continue blending until you reach your desired consistency.

4. Taste the hummus and adjust the seasoning with more salt or lemon juice if needed. You can also adjust the thickness by adding more water if desired.

Serve the Hummus:

5. Transfer the hummus to a serving bowl.

6. Drizzle extra-virgin olive oil over the top and sprinkle with paprika, chopped fresh parsley, pine nuts, or olives for garnish, if desired.

7. Serve the hummus with pita bread, fresh vegetables, crackers, or as a dip for your favorite snacks.

8. Enjoy your homemade hummus!

Hummus is a versatile dip that can be customized to your taste. You can experiment with additional flavors like roasted red pepper, sun-dried tomato, or herbs to create your own unique variations.

Bunny Chow (South Africa)

Bunny Chow is a South African street food dish consisting of a hollowed-out loaf of bread filled with curry. It's a flavorful and comforting dish that's popular in South Africa. Here's a recipe for Chicken Bunny Chow:

Ingredients:

For the Curry:

- 1.5 pounds (about 680g) boneless, skinless chicken thighs or breast, cut into bite-sized pieces
- 2 tablespoons vegetable oil
- 1 large onion, chopped
- 2 cloves garlic, minced
- 1-inch piece of ginger, minced
- 2 tablespoons curry powder (adjust to your spice preference)
- 1 teaspoon ground cumin
- 1 teaspoon ground coriander
- 1 teaspoon ground paprika
- 1/2 teaspoon ground turmeric
- 1/4 teaspoon cayenne pepper (adjust to your spice preference)
- 1 can (14 oz or 400g) diced tomatoes
- 1 can (14 oz or 400g) chickpeas, drained and rinsed
- 1 cup chicken broth or water
- Salt and black pepper, to taste
- Fresh cilantro leaves, chopped (for garnish)

For the Bunny Chow:

- 4 small round bread rolls or hollowed-out bread loaves (such as French bread)
- Butter, for spreading (optional)

Instructions:

Prepare the Curry:

1. In a large skillet or pan, heat the vegetable oil over medium heat.
2. Add chopped onions and sauté until they become translucent, about 3-5 minutes.
3. Stir in minced garlic and ginger, and cook for another 1-2 minutes until fragrant.
4. Add the chicken pieces and cook until they are no longer pink on the outside.

5. Add the curry powder, ground cumin, ground coriander, ground paprika, ground turmeric, and cayenne pepper to the pan. Stir well to coat the chicken with the spices.

6. Pour in the diced tomatoes (with their juice) and chickpeas. Stir to combine.

7. Add chicken broth (or water) to the pan and season with salt and black pepper. Bring the mixture to a simmer.

8. Cover and let it simmer for about 15-20 minutes or until the chicken is cooked through and the sauce has thickened. Stir occasionally.

Prepare the Bunny Chow:

9. While the curry is simmering, prepare the bread rolls or loaves. Cut off the top portion of each roll or loaf and hollow out the center to create a bread "bowl." You can spread butter on the inside if you like.

10. Once the curry is ready, ladle it into the hollowed-out bread rolls or loaves.

11. Garnish with fresh cilantro leaves.

12. Place the bread tops back on as "lids" or serve them on the side.

13. Serve the Chicken Bunny Chow immediately.

Enjoy your homemade South African Chicken Bunny Chow, a delightful fusion of flavors and textures!

S u y a   (N i g e r i a)

Suya is a popular Nigerian street food dish consisting of skewered and grilled meat, usually beef or chicken, that's seasoned with a flavorful peanut-based spice mix. It's a tasty and spicy treat often served with onions, tomatoes, and a spicy peanut sauce. Here's a recipe for Chicken Suya:

Ingredients:

For the Chicken:

- 1 pound (about 450g) boneless, skinless chicken breasts or thighs, cut into small, bite-sized pieces
- Wooden skewers, soaked in water for 30 minutes

For the Suya Spice Mix:

- 1/2 cup roasted unsalted peanuts
- 2 tablespoons ground cayenne pepper (adjust to your spice preference)
- 1 tablespoon ground paprika
- 1 teaspoon ground ginger
- 1 teaspoon ground garlic
- 1 teaspoon onion powder
- 1/2 teaspoon ground cumin
- 1/2 teaspoon ground coriander
- 1/2 teaspoon ground nutmeg
- Salt, to taste
- 2 tablespoons vegetable oil

For Serving:

- Sliced red onions
- Sliced tomatoes
- Spicy peanut sauce (recipe below)

Instructions:

Prepare the Suya Spice Mix:

1. In a food processor or blender, combine roasted peanuts, ground cayenne pepper, ground paprika, ground ginger, ground garlic, onion powder, ground cumin, ground coriander, ground nutmeg, and salt. Blend until you have a fine powder.
2. Transfer the spice mix to a bowl and stir in the vegetable oil. This will create a paste-like consistency. Adjust the seasoning to your taste.

Marinate and Skewer the Chicken:

3. Thread the chicken pieces onto the soaked wooden skewers, ensuring they are evenly distributed.

4. Coat the chicken skewers with the Suya spice mix, pressing it onto the meat to adhere.

5. Place the skewers on a plate, cover with plastic wrap, and refrigerate for at least 30 minutes to allow the flavors to marinate.

Grill the Chicken Suya:

6. Preheat your grill to medium-high heat.

7. Grill the chicken skewers for about 4-5 minutes per side, or until the chicken is cooked through and has a nice char. Cooking times may vary depending on the thickness of the chicken.

Serve the Chicken Suya:

8. Remove the chicken skewers from the grill.

9. Serve the Chicken Suya hot with sliced red onions, sliced tomatoes, and spicy peanut sauce (recipe below) on the side.

Spicy Peanut Sauce:

Ingredients:

- 1/2 cup roasted unsalted peanuts

- 1 clove garlic

- 1-2 small red or green chilies (adjust to your spice preference)

- 2 tablespoons vegetable oil

- 1 tablespoon lemon juice

- 1 teaspoon soy sauce

- Salt, to taste

- Water, as needed

Instructions:

1. In a blender or food processor, combine roasted peanuts, garlic, chilies, vegetable oil, lemon juice, soy sauce, and a pinch of salt.

2. Blend until the mixture becomes smooth, adding a little water as needed to achieve your desired consistency.

3. Taste and adjust the seasoning, adding more salt or lemon juice if necessary.

4. Serve the spicy peanut sauce alongside the Chicken Suya for dipping.

Enjoy your homemade Chicken Suya, a flavorful and spicy Nigerian street food delight!

Meat Pie (Australia)

Meat Pie is a classic Australian comfort food consisting of a savory meat filling encased in flaky pastry. It's often enjoyed as a hand-held snack or meal. Here's a recipe for traditional Australian Meat Pies:

Ingredients:

For the Meat Filling:

- 1 pound (about 450g) ground beef or minced beef
- 1 onion, finely chopped
- 2 cloves garlic, minced
- 1 carrot, finely diced
- 1 celery stalk, finely diced
- 1 cup frozen peas
- 2 tablespoons tomato paste
- 1 tablespoon Worcestershire sauce
- 1 teaspoon dried thyme
- 1 teaspoon dried rosemary
- Salt and black pepper, to taste
- 1 cup beef broth
- 2 tablespoons all-purpose flour
- 2 tablespoons vegetable oil

For the Pastry:

- 2 sheets of store-bought puff pastry, thawed
- 1 egg, beaten (for egg wash)

Instructions:

Prepare the Meat Filling:

1. In a large skillet or frying pan, heat the vegetable oil over medium heat.
2. Add the chopped onion, minced garlic, diced carrot, and diced celery. Sauté for about 5 minutes until the vegetables start to soften.
3. Add the ground beef and cook, breaking it apart with a spoon, until it's browned and cooked through.
4. Stir in the tomato paste, Worcestershire sauce, dried thyme, dried rosemary, salt, and black pepper. Cook for a few more minutes to allow the flavors to meld.

5. Sprinkle the flour over the meat mixture and stir to combine. This will help thicken the filling.

6. Pour in the beef broth and stir until the mixture thickens into a gravy-like consistency.

7. Add the frozen peas and cook for another 2-3 minutes until they are heated through.

8. Remove the pan from heat and let the meat filling cool slightly.

Assemble and Bake the Meat Pies:

9. Preheat your oven to 375°F (190°C).

10. Lay out one sheet of puff pastry on a clean, floured surface. Cut it into four equal squares.

11. Place a generous spoonful of the meat filling in the center of each pastry square.

12. Beat the egg in a small bowl and use it to brush the edges of the pastry.

13. Fold the pastry over the filling to create a triangle or rectangle shape. Press the edges together to seal the pies. You can use a fork to crimp the edges for a decorative touch.

14. Transfer the assembled meat pies to a baking sheet lined with parchment paper.

15. Brush the tops of the pies with more beaten egg for a golden finish.

Bake the Meat Pies:

16. Bake the meat pies in the preheated oven for about 20-25 minutes, or until they are puffed up and golden brown.

17. Remove the pies from the oven and let them cool slightly before serving.

Serve the Meat Pies:

18. Enjoy your homemade Australian Meat Pies warm as a snack or meal. They can be served with tomato sauce (ketchup) on the side, if desired.

These delicious Meat Pies are a beloved Australian classic, perfect for any occasion!

Lamingtons (Australia)

Lamingtons are a classic Australian dessert consisting of squares of sponge cake coated in a layer of chocolate icing and desiccated coconut. They are a beloved treat often enjoyed with a cup of tea or coffee. Here's a recipe for homemade Lamingtons:

Ingredients:

For the Sponge Cake:

- 2 cups all-purpose flour
- 2 teaspoons baking powder
- 1/4 teaspoon salt
- 1/2 cup unsalted butter, softened
- 1 cup granulated sugar
- 2 large eggs
- 1 teaspoon vanilla extract
- 1/2 cup milk

For the Chocolate Icing:

- 2 cups powdered sugar (icing sugar)
- 1/3 cup unsweetened cocoa powder
- 2 tablespoons unsalted butter, melted
- 1/2 cup milk

For Coating:

- 2 cups desiccated coconut

Instructions:

Prepare the Sponge Cake:

1. Preheat your oven to 350°F (180°C). Grease and line a 9x9-inch (23x23 cm) square cake pan with parchment paper, leaving some overhang for easy removal.

2. In a bowl, whisk together the flour, baking powder, and salt. Set aside.

3. In a separate large mixing bowl, cream together the softened butter and granulated sugar until light and fluffy, which takes about 2-3 minutes.

4. Add the eggs, one at a time, beating well after each addition. Stir in the vanilla extract.

5. Gradually add the dry ingredients to the wet mixture, alternating with the milk, beginning and ending with the dry ingredients. Mix until just combined. Do not overmix.

6. Pour the cake batter into the prepared pan and smooth the top.

7. Bake in the preheated oven for about 25-30 minutes, or until a toothpick inserted into the center comes out clean.

8. Remove the cake from the oven and let it cool in the pan for about 10 minutes. Then, use the parchment paper overhangs to lift the cake out of the pan and onto a wire rack to cool completely.

Prepare the Chocolate Icing and Coat the Lamingtons:

9. In a bowl, sift together the powdered sugar and cocoa powder.

10. Add the melted butter and milk to the cocoa mixture, and whisk until you have a smooth and glossy chocolate icing.

11. Cut the cooled sponge cake into small squares or rectangles, about 2x2 inches (5x5 cm).

12. Dip each cake square into the chocolate icing, making sure it's well-coated. Allow any excess icing to drip off.

13. Roll the chocolate-coated cake square in desiccated coconut until it's evenly coated. You can gently press the coconut onto the cake if needed.

14. Place the coated Lamingtons on a wire rack to set. Repeat this process for all the cake squares.

Serve the Lamingtons:

15. Let the Lamingtons sit for a few hours or overnight to allow the icing to set and the flavors to meld.

16. Serve your homemade Lamingtons with a hot cup of tea or coffee and enjoy this iconic Australian dessert!

Lamingtons are a delightful treat, perfect for special occasions or whenever you're in the mood for a sweet and coconut-chocolatey indulgence.

Jamaican Jerk Chicken

Jamaican Jerk Chicken is a flavorful and spicy grilled or roasted chicken dish that's marinated in a vibrant and aromatic jerk seasoning mixture. The jerk marinade typically includes a combination of Scotch bonnet peppers, allspice (pimento), garlic, ginger, thyme, and various spices. Here's a recipe for homemade Jamaican Jerk Chicken:

Ingredients:

For the Jerk Marinade:

- 2-3 Scotch bonnet peppers (adjust to your spice preference; wear gloves when handling)

- 3-4 cloves garlic, minced

- 1 small onion, chopped

- 2-3 green onions, chopped

- 1 thumb-sized piece of fresh ginger, minced

- 2 tablespoons fresh thyme leaves (or 2 teaspoons dried thyme)

- 1 tablespoon ground allspice (pimento)

- 1 teaspoon ground cinnamon

- 1/2 teaspoon ground nutmeg

- 1/2 teaspoon ground cloves

- 2 tablespoons soy sauce

- 2 tablespoons vegetable oil

- Juice of 2 limes

- Salt and black pepper, to taste

For the Chicken:

- 4-6 bone-in, skin-on chicken pieces (such as thighs and drumsticks)

- Vegetable oil for grilling or roasting

Instructions:

Prepare the Jerk Marinade:

1. In a food processor or blender, combine the Scotch bonnet peppers (seeds and all), minced garlic, chopped onion, chopped green onions, minced ginger, fresh thyme leaves, ground allspice, ground cinnamon, ground nutmeg, ground cloves, soy sauce, vegetable oil, lime juice, salt, and black pepper.

2. Blend the ingredients until you have a smooth and thick paste. You may need to scrape down the sides of the blender or food processor to ensure everything is well combined.

Marinate the Chicken:

3. Make shallow cuts or scores in the chicken pieces to allow the marinade to penetrate.

4. Place the chicken pieces in a large bowl or resealable plastic bag and pour the jerk marinade over them. Use your hands to massage the marinade into the chicken, ensuring it's well coated.

5. Seal the bowl or bag and refrigerate the marinated chicken for at least 4 hours, or preferably overnight, to let the flavors develop.

Grill or Roast the Jerk Chicken:

6. Preheat your grill to medium-high heat or preheat your oven to 375°F (190°C).

7. If grilling, oil the grill grates to prevent sticking. If roasting, place a wire rack on a baking sheet and lightly oil it.

8. Remove the marinated chicken from the refrigerator and let it come to room temperature for about 30 minutes before cooking.

9. Grill or roast the chicken for about 20-30 minutes, turning occasionally, until it's cooked through and has a nice char on the outside. The internal temperature of the chicken should reach 165°F (74°C).

Serve the Jamaican Jerk Chicken:

10. Remove the chicken from the grill or oven and let it rest for a few minutes before serving.

11. Serve your homemade Jamaican Jerk Chicken with traditional accompaniments like rice and peas, fried plantains, and coleslaw. You can also drizzle any remaining jerk marinade over the chicken for extra flavor.

Enjoy the bold and spicy flavors of Jamaican Jerk Chicken, a delicious and iconic dish from the Caribbean!

Roti (Trinidad and Tobago)

Roti is a popular Trinidadian and Tobagonian dish that consists of unleavened flatbread served with a variety of fillings or curries. It's a versatile and delicious meal that can be made with different types of fillings, such as chicken, beef, goat, shrimp, or vegetables. Here's a recipe for Trinidadian Chicken Roti:

Ingredients:

For the Roti Dough:

- 3 cups all-purpose flour

- 1 teaspoon salt

- 1 cup water

- 2 tablespoons vegetable oil

For the Chicken Curry Filling:

- 1 pound (about 450g) boneless, skinless chicken thighs or breast, cut into small pieces

- 2 tablespoons vegetable oil

- 1 onion, chopped

- 3 cloves garlic, minced

- 1 tablespoon curry powder (adjust to your spice preference)

- 1 teaspoon ground cumin

- 1 teaspoon ground coriander

- 1 teaspoon ground turmeric

- 1/2 teaspoon ground cayenne pepper (adjust to your spice preference)

- Salt and black pepper, to taste

- 1 can (14 oz or 400g) diced tomatoes

- 1 cup chicken broth

- 2 medium potatoes, peeled and diced

- 1 cup diced carrots

- 1 cup diced bell peppers (red and green)

- 1 cup diced pumpkin (optional)

- Chopped fresh cilantro or parsley, for garnish (optional)

Instructions:

Prepare the Roti Dough:

1. In a large mixing bowl, combine the all-purpose flour and salt.

2. Gradually add water while mixing until a dough forms. Knead the dough for about 5-10 minutes until it's smooth and elastic.

3. Divide the dough into 6 equal portions and roll each portion into a ball.

4. Brush each dough ball with vegetable oil, cover them, and let them rest for at least 30 minutes.

Prepare the Chicken Curry Filling:

5. In a large skillet or frying pan, heat vegetable oil over medium heat.

6. Add chopped onions and sauté until they become translucent, about 3-5 minutes.

7. Stir in minced garlic, curry powder, ground cumin, ground coriander, ground turmeric, ground cayenne pepper, salt, and black pepper. Cook for 2 minutes, stirring constantly, until fragrant.

8. Add the chicken pieces and cook until they are browned on all sides.

9. Pour in the diced tomatoes (with their juice) and chicken broth. Stir to combine.

10. Add diced potatoes and carrots. Simmer for about 10-15 minutes until the potatoes and carrots are tender and the chicken is cooked through.

11. Stir in diced bell peppers and diced pumpkin (if using). Cook for another 5-7 minutes until the vegetables are tender but still crisp.

Assemble and Serve the Chicken Roti:

12. While the filling is cooking, roll out each of the rested dough balls into thin rounds, about 6-8 inches (15-20 cm) in diameter.

13. Heat a griddle or non-stick skillet over medium-high heat. Place a dough round on the griddle and cook until it puffs up and has golden brown spots on both sides. Repeat for all the dough rounds.

14. To serve, place a roti round on a plate and spoon some of the chicken curry filling onto the center. Fold the sides of the roti over the filling to create a parcel.

15. Garnish with chopped fresh cilantro or parsley, if desired.

16. Serve your homemade Trinidadian Chicken Roti immediately and enjoy!

Trinidadian Chicken Roti is a hearty and flavorful dish that combines tender chicken curry with soft, chewy roti bread. It's a beloved street food in Trinidad and Tobago and a delightful meal for any occasion.

Sausage Roll (UK/Australia)

Sausage rolls are a popular savory pastry snack in the UK and Australia. They consist of seasoned ground meat (typically sausage meat) wrapped in flaky puff pastry. Sausage rolls are often enjoyed as a finger food, party snack, or quick meal. Here's a recipe for homemade sausage rolls:

Ingredients:

- 1 pound (about 450g) ground pork sausage meat (you can also use ground beef, turkey, or a combination)
- 1/2 small onion, finely chopped
- 1 clove garlic, minced
- 1/2 teaspoon dried sage
- 1/2 teaspoon dried thyme
- Salt and black pepper, to taste
- 1 sheet of frozen puff pastry, thawed
- 1 egg, beaten (for egg wash)

Instructions:

Prepare the Sausage Filling:

1. In a mixing bowl, combine the ground pork sausage meat, finely chopped onion, minced garlic, dried sage, dried thyme, salt, and black pepper. Mix until the seasonings are evenly distributed throughout the meat.

Assemble the Sausage Rolls:

2. Preheat your oven to 400°F (200°C) and line a baking sheet with parchment paper.
3. Roll out the thawed puff pastry sheet on a lightly floured surface to create a rectangle. Cut it in half lengthwise to make two long strips.
4. Divide the sausage mixture into two equal portions.
5. Place one portion of the sausage mixture along the center of each puff pastry strip, forming a long sausage-like shape.
6. Fold one edge of the puff pastry over the sausage mixture, and then fold the other edge over to encase the sausage entirely. Press the edges together to seal.
7. Use a sharp knife to cut each long roll into smaller pieces, about 2-3 inches (5-7 cm) long. You can make them shorter or longer based on your preference.

Bake the Sausage Rolls:

8. Place the sausage roll pieces on the prepared baking sheet, leaving some space between each roll.
9. Brush the tops of the sausage rolls with beaten egg to give them a shiny, golden finish.

10. Bake in the preheated oven for about 20-25 minutes or until the sausage rolls are puffed up and have turned golden brown.

11. Remove the sausage rolls from the oven and let them cool for a few minutes before serving.

Serve the Sausage Rolls:

12. Sausage rolls are typically enjoyed warm. They can be served as a snack, appetizer, or part of a meal.

13. Serve your homemade sausage rolls with ketchup, mustard, or your favorite dipping sauce.

Enjoy your homemade UK and Australian-style sausage rolls, a delicious and comforting snack or treat!

Samgyeopsal (Korean BBQ)

Samgyeopsal is a popular Korean dish known as "Korean BBQ." It consists of thick slices of pork belly that are grilled at the table, typically on a charcoal or gas grill. Samgyeopsal is often enjoyed with a variety of side dishes and condiments. Here's how to prepare and enjoy this delicious Korean BBQ at home:

Ingredients:

For the Samgyeopsal:

- 1 pound (about 450g) thick-cut pork belly slices
- Vegetable oil (for greasing the grill)

For the Dipping Sauces (Ssamjang and Sesame Oil with Salt):

- Ssamjang (a Korean dipping sauce made from fermented soybean paste and red pepper paste, available at Korean grocery stores)
- Sesame oil
- Salt

For Serving:

- Fresh lettuce leaves (for wrapping)
- Fresh perilla leaves (optional, for wrapping)
- Sliced garlic cloves
- Sliced green chilies (optional, for those who like it spicy)
- Sliced scallions
- Kimchi (fermented spicy cabbage)
- Pickled radishes (danmuji)
- Fresh or pickled vegetables like cucumber, carrots, and peppers

Instructions:

Prepare the Grill:

1. If using a tabletop Korean BBQ grill, place it on the table and preheat it according to the manufacturer's instructions. If you don't have a tabletop grill, you can also use a stovetop grill pan or an outdoor grill.

Grill the Samgyeopsal:

2. Lightly grease the grill with vegetable oil to prevent sticking.
3. Place the pork belly slices on the preheated grill. You can also grill some sliced garlic and green chilies alongside the pork for added flavor.

4. Grill the pork slices for about 2-3 minutes per side, or until they are cooked through and have a nice char and crispiness on the outside. Cooking times may vary depending on the thickness of the slices and the heat of the grill.

Prepare the Dipping Sauces:

5. While the pork is grilling, prepare the dipping sauces. One dipping sauce is made by mixing ssamjang with a bit of sesame oil. The other dipping sauce is simply sesame oil with a pinch of salt. Adjust the proportions to your taste.

Serve the Samgyeopsal:

6. To eat samgyeopsal, take a lettuce leaf or perilla leaf (if using) and place a slice of grilled pork inside.

7. Add your choice of sliced garlic, green chilies, scallions, and any other condiments you like.

8. Top it off with a small amount of the ssamjang and sesame oil with salt dipping sauces.

9. Wrap the ingredients in the lettuce or perilla leaf and eat it in one bite for a burst of flavors and textures.

10. Enjoy your homemade Korean BBQ experience with a variety of side dishes and condiments.

Samgyeopsal is often enjoyed as a communal meal, making it a fun and interactive dining experience. Gather your friends or family around the grill, and enjoy the delicious flavors of Korean BBQ together.